Dancing
With
Demons

by Riley Ivanitski

This story is dedicated to Mrs. Whorton and Mr. O'Halloran.
Thank you for the overwhelming amount of support and inspiration, along with much needed guidance.

Prologue

September 17th, 2004

Dear Mama,

It's CoCo. Aunt Val says you aren't coming back, but Aunt Val says a lot of things. She doesn't know you the way I do, nobody does. No matter how much I tell her that you'll be back for my birthday, she never seems to believe me. Vermont is so different from Nashville. I miss the heat and I miss the diner. Of course, I miss you the most though.

I have so many questions to ask but I'm saving them for the day that we're together again. For now, though, I'll send you letters because I know you're missing me just as much as I'm missing you. I could really use a warm, Nashville style bear hug right about now.

While I miss Tennessee, Vermont is a beauty. I won't get comfortable here, though. I know you'll be here soon. I don't want to get used to things that won't stick around.

Tomorrow I have to start going to a group. Aunt Val told me it would help me learn how to move on. I don't know what I'm moving on from, though. Aunt Val must be saying something wacky again, just like she always does. I can't wait to hear your stories and I can't wait for you to hear mine.

I hope to see you on my birthday next week, so we can watch *Wizard of Oz* and order from the diner, even though the diner is far now and Aunt Val only has old DVDs of *Punky Brewster.*

Oodles of love,

Cove Collins

Table of Contents

Bushels of Love, Cove

September 22nd, 2004

Dear Mom,

Vermont is nothing like Tennessee. People at school aren't nice, but that's okay. They say my accent is never going to get me a job, but that's okay. I started going to the group I was telling you about. I still don't know why I have to go, something about helping me adapt social skills or something. I don't need them, though.

There was a real pretty girl there, though. I guess that's why I'm learning how to talk to people, so I can talk to people like her. She has this long and silky brown hair and these burnt out purple ends that reminded me of the purple faded silk picture frame that held the first picture of you and me when I was born. I know it's weird to connect

1

things like hair and picture frames, but Mr. Graves said to relate people's traits to things that are important to you. Mr. Graves is my group advisor. Mr. Graves smells the way Daddy did when he came home from work. Freshly printed newspapers and groceries. Hopefully this group is as beneficial as Aunt Val says it'll be. I want to be friends with the girl with pretty hair.

My birthday is only two days away, I hope to see you there. I'm visiting Daddy to talk to him for a little bit in the morning and then Aunt Val said we can go to Blockbuster and pick out a few movies or CDs to watch that night. I'll be sure to pick up *Wizard of Oz.*

Bushels of love,

Your soon to be not so little CoCo

September 23rd, 2004

Dear Mama, ,

Aunt Val gave me my early birthday present today, even though I wanted to open it tomorrow. She got me the bike I've been asking you for since I was 14. The one you said I wouldn't use. The wrapping paper on it was dusty, so it must have been around for a while and I just didn't know. Sneaky Aunt Val. She gave me that bike so I can ride it to the church for group. Maybe I can show the girl with pretty hair my new bike. The lavender ribbon laced through the wicker basket in the front reminds me of her hair. I told Aunt Val about her. She says I need to be more observant and find out what her name is. Aunt Val said I should see if she wants to come over for cake and Italian take out

Tomorrow. I asked Aunt Val if we can put a birthday candle in the garlic knot because I wanted it to be like when you put a candle in a matzo ball from my soup when we ordered from the diner. All she did was make a confused face. She'll never understand.

Hopefully Mr. Graves can help me get rid of the people that dance in my head. Aunt Val calls them demons. I think that seems a little scary, so I say I'm dancing with demons. Every time I mention them to Aunt Val, she makes the confused face again. I guess it's just another one of those things that she'll never understand.

I can't wait for you to meet the girl whose name I don't know yet I feel a connection to. Hopefully you get here before Aunt Val leaves to pick up the food, I wouldn't want her to forget that you like your chicken parm with light sauce. It's been so long, I can't wait to see you.

Bushels of love,

17 and 364/365 years old Cove

September 24th, 2004

Dear Mama,,

Today was good. Really good. The girl with the pretty hair is named Vera. Vera's dad is in the military, but I forgot what branch. She's 19 and lives in an old Volkswagen van that she painted light pink. She has the ability to leave and drive out of this town but she said that she just knows that the universe wants her here. Vera hasn't gotten the chance to write to her dad yet, but I'm sure he'd love to hear from her just like you love hearing from me, even though your letters are getting lost in the mail. This morning I had cereal for breakfast before we visited Daddy. Aunt Val put sprinkles in my Rice Krispies and got me a pin for my jacket that says, "Cheers to 18 years." with a picture of a little cactus on it because she knows succulents are my favorite.

Aunt Val suggested that she waits in the car while I talk to Daddy. She went on about how it's been too long and how he doesn't want to see her. Even though I tried my best to tell her that isn't true, and that Daddy was never the kind of man to hold a grudge, she sighed and reached her arm across the car to open my door.

I closed the car door and blew a kiss to Aunt Val, I knew she would be waiting for a while. I sat down criss cross in front of Daddy and started to pick the grass in front of him as I started rambling. I told him everything he's missed since Father's Day. I told him about Vera. I told him I was going to get to see you today and that Aunt Val said hi. I sat and talked to him for about an hour, but then Aunt Val gestured for me to head back to the car. I told you how much I missed you and wiped underneath my eyes. I reapplied the red lipstick I took off the bathroom sink before we left and kissed the empty space next to his name. The stone was extraordinarily cold today and the morning dew hadn't been absorbed by the stone all the way yet, but the red lipstick was especially opaque today, which means Daddy felt it.

Aunt Val and I went to Blockbuster after that. I wanted to tell her what I told Daddy, but I didn't want to hurt her heart the way it seems I hurt yours. When we got to Blockbuster, I picked out the Wizard of Oz before I forgot and then went to the Disney movies. I picked out whatever they had left and Aunt Val and I left. When we got back home, Vera was parked outside with a happy birthday banner hanging from her van. I ran up to her and hugged her. The last person I hugged was Daddy. Vera told me her last hug was from her dad as well. Aunt Val had a Cheshire Cat smile on her face, which was fitting since Alice in Wonderland was the movie she picked out. Vera and I both ordered the fettuccini alfredo and I asked Aunt Val to get your chicken parm with light sauce, because I knew you'd be running late like you always do. I didn't mind sharing my garlic bread with Vera.

When we were done eating, Aunt Val almost put on *Wizard of Oz* without you there, don't worry though, I stopped her just in time. She then put on *Beauty and the Beast*. Personally, I think Vera looks just like Belle. She has the same soft voice and patience as her too. After *Beauty and the Beast*, Aunt Val brought out the cake. It was a white cake with strawberry frosting, just like Daddy would make for me. It was amazing. I wrapped a piece in foil and put it in the fridge for you, it's next to your chicken parm. I don't think they put light sauce on it, they never seem to remember to.

Aunt Val extended the rental of *Wizard of Oz* because I couldn't watch it without you. I put the DVD for it on top of the fridge. Since I'm the only one that can reach up there, Aunt Val won't be able to return it. Don't worry, I'll wait for you. Vera can come over again and eat leftover cake with us and watch Wizard of Oz, she appreciates things like that.

Love,

Your now adult baby Cove

Love,
Vera

September 25, 2004

Dear Daddy,

I know this letter is long overdue. I wanted to write to you everytime something bad happened in my life, and bad things just kept happening. Although it took me a while to gather the strength to tell you, I'm finally ready. About 7 months ago, right around the time you left, I guess Mama wasn't able to handle your absence as well as she cared to admit. I would go to sleep without her being home, and wake up without her home or possibly tumbling through the door with bruises on her forearms. I would come home from school and she would be passed out on the couch, with an array of Red Solo cups around her. She stopped going to work, and stopped caring about anything all together. It was incredible to me that we still had the house, but I couldn't speak to her about these things without her telling me how useless and ungrateful I was. I wish you were there to see the look of sheer frustration in her face. It was like she hated me. I also wish Emily was here, she would've helped keep Mama calmed down.

Mama slowly started to become less and less coherent. Her skin started turning a pale yellow, and I was terrified. Even though there were only a few months left of school, I dropped out. Mama needed as much help as she could get. I tried my best to get her back to where she needed to be. Nothing was working. Daddy please forgive me because I tried my hardest but Mama would always go back to her old ways.

I went to the grocery one day and when I returned, Mama had her clothes nicely folded on the toilet seat and she was in the tub, yellow as could be, eyes wide open. I was at a loss for words since I didn't have anyone physically there for me anymore. I failed her, I failed you, I failed Emily. Emily and Mama were always so close, you know that. Emily is looking down at me mighty disappointed right now. After Mama was removed from our home, I sold all of our furniture and Mama's clothes. I kept your important things, like your favorite flannel and your suit from Emily's funeral. The only thing of Emily's I kept was the other half of our matching lockets that say "until the end." Even though her end already happened, I'm not ready to let go of it yet.

After I sold all of our furniture, I took the bus to Uncle Roger's car dealership a few towns away and bought the last Volkswagen van they had with the small amount of money I had. He asked how Mama was doing, I told him that she passed away from a heart attack to avoid a lecture. He offered for me to stay with him and Granny, but I told him I needed time to myself. He wanted me to explain to you that he is so proud of you, and that if Granny understood where you were, then she would be just as proud. Uncle Roger said that he could help me fix up that van with some leftover light pink paint that he had from when he was painting the baby's room. That reminds me, he also wanted me to tell you that she didn't end up making it, and Aunt Kim didn't want to be with him after they lost her.

When we made my new van all pink and fixed up some rusty parts. Uncle Roger insisted on me staying for dinner and that I'm all Granny ever talks about. When he got off from work, I saved him a few dollars and drove him home so he didn't have to take the bus. When we got there, the house smelled like mildew and Granny was sitting in her recliner with the oxygen tank on her side. I made eye contact with her and smiled. She kept cocking her head to make sure it was me.

"My beautiful Emily!" Granny said with the most confidence. It shattered my heart but I didn't have the courage to tell her that I was Vera. "Oh, my beautiful girl, how I've missed you! Your hair grew back so quickly since the last time I saw you, and the scar on your neck cleared up!" I could feel my eyes welling up and my lip beginning to quiver from trying to hold it back. I didn't say anything, I just rested my hand on her cheek and kissed her forehead. I looked back at Uncle Roger as my tears became more apparent. He looked choked up as well and slowly nodded. I looked at Granny one last time and gave Uncle Roger a big ole hug on my way out the door. While I was hugging him, I slipped as much money as I was able to into his pocket. I think it was about 150, so I hope he uses it for all the right reasons.

I drove back home that night and started playing some of your old Pink Floyd CDs. I miss you so much. When I think about how long it's been since I've spoken to you hurts me more than you know. With that being said, I hope the cramps I keep getting in my hands are worth it, and that you truly understand how much I wish you were here right now.

By the time everything happened with Mama and I got situated with my van, it was about mid-August. One day, I had to stock up on food again, but this time I went to the farmers market. Also, since I was running low on money, I desperately needed a job. By this time, I was so content with my lifestyle, I didn't want to give it up. When I got to the farmers market, our old neighbor Mr. Graves was handing out samples of apple slices. I didn't recognize him at first, but once I heard his scratchy voice calling for me, I knew it was him.

"VeeBee!" he said with the utmost joy. I

jogged over to him and I knew his smile was genuine because the wrinkles in his cheeks became clearer. He asked how "his favorite Barons'" were doing. I simply told him that we were down another member and that with you in the Marines I was living on my own. He told me how strong I was and how I get it from you. He told me that after he retired, he started working at the farmers market on the weekend for a few extra dollars to help him and his cat get by. He also told me about a support group he started for young adults to help them branch out and help structure their future. He asked how long it had been since I spoke to people my age, and although it took all of my strength, I admitted that the last person was Emily. The most vivid moment from this conversation was the way his mustache frowned with his mouth. It reminded me of you, although I'm sure you aren't allowed to have your mustache anymore.

When he was explaining the purpose of the group, I didn't think it sounded like my scene. I told him that I'd go to the next one to see how I like it and I'll make my next decision after that, he was thrilled. When I also explained to him the van life and how I was looking for a job, he said he would see what he could do to help. Long story short, now I work at the farmers market. It's only three days a week working at the food stalls, but one day a week I bring Pops' old guitar with me to play for some tips.

I started my first day two days after speaking to Mr. Graves. After the end of my shift, I began getting ready for the group. The group met in a church basement every few days, it always varied on how Mr. Graves was feeling. When I walked into the room, there was a strange ominous vibe that made me uncomfortable. The fluorescent lights beaming off of the linoleum tile reminded me of Emily's hospital room, I guess that was what made it so uncomfortable. I sat down in the circle of seats and across from me was a girl with the most freckled face I've ever seen. Her eyes were emerald, just like Mama and Emily's. She has unnaturally short and choppy blonde hair. Every time we made eye contact, she would abruptly look down at the ground and begin anxiously twiddling her thumbs. Thank goodness we were there to learn how to talk to people otherwise we would have never spoken.

The second meeting I went to, she came up to me and asked my name. Before I could finish saying it, she asked if I wanted to go to her house for her birthday. Of course I said yes because I figured everyone would be proud of me for actually talking to people instead of sulking.

The girl's name was Cove, and although she seemed odd, odd is good and I welcomed it. She pays attention to detail, I was able to tell because she kept staring at the burnt out purple ends of my hair. That's an indicator of how long it's been since I've seen you. The day you left my hair was bright purple. I don't have the heart to either cut it or dye it again because the last time you told me you loved me before you left, you complimented my hair and reminded me that purple was Emily's favorite color.

I'm sorry I keep rambling about Emily. I guess I never comprehended her death until I was alone. I felt a connection with Cove, though. I know, very hippie of me. When her birthday finally came, I waited in the parking lot of her apartment complex. Since I was pretty early, I decided to try and make a banner for her birthday made of the few craft supplies I had. I opened up the side door and taped the banner in the corners. I sat around on my own for a little while, but I was okay with it because that's when I was figuring out how to start this letter for you.

When they finally came back, I helped them bring in bags of food and bags from Blockbuster that contained movies Cove couldn't wait to show me. When we got in their apartment, it was so cozy, something I wasn't used to. Well, at least since Emily's been gone. I was helping her aunt unpack the food and there was an extra container that Cove made sure nobody else ate, I guess she's passionate about her chicken parmesan.

Cove and her aunt rented about 5 Disney movies. I loved every single one of them. Cove was ecstatic the whole time I was there. She didn't want me to leave, though. I missed the feeling of someone wanting me around, but at the same time I knew someone hurt her to make her feel this way. It was humbling. I know the speed of our friendship seems weird, but it almost felt like we've known each other for years. I know I'll still see her at our group, but I'd love to get to know her more. I could use a friend more than anything right now.

The main reason I'm so hesitant to show Cove how I feel is because I always get hurt by storing too much faith into people. I can't let that happen again. I'm trying my best to stay positive. Mr. Graves has done nothing but spread positivity during the group meetings, so hopefully they help me out as much as he thinks it will.

I'm picking Cove up tomorrow so we can hang out. I need to get a better understanding of why we feel so connected. Lastly, Cove's aunt said that I can use their address for you to send letters back to me. If you don't want to write back to me, I completely understand where you're coming from, I wouldn't want to talk to me right now either.

Love,

Vera Baron

Unapologetically,
Cove

September 27, 2004

Dear Mama,

We had to throw your food away. The whole fridge started to smell like chicken parmesan. I asked Aunt Val if we could get you some more or even make it on our own, but she said we couldn't. I swear I need to talk to the darn mailman about these letters. You would've known to be here by now if the letters didn't keep getting lost. I really don't remember the last time I saw you, it feels like years. It feels like I went to sleep tucked in my bed in Nashville and woke up on Aunt Val's couch in Vermont.

Yesterday I saw Vera. We went to the farmers market that she works at because she wanted me to watch her play her guitar for some extra money so we could get something to eat afterward. I can't help but think about her outfit that day. It was so plain, but a pretty plain. She had her hair down with pieces of the top pinned back. She had a short sleeved white shirt on with a black tank top over it. I remember how much you didn't like when I did that, but once you meet Vera you'll understand why it's different for her to wear it. She also had a pair of loose jeans on. She told me she had to wear them because she had to do her laundry and had to wear her dad's pants. I had some change that Aunt Val gave me for snacks from the store, but I threw all of it into Vera's open guitar case so we could go to a laundromat.

When I did this, she was still tuning her guitar, so she just looked confused, but I pointed at my pants so she would know what I meant. She smirked and kept tuning her guitar. Since I still had a few minutes before she started her mini performance, I started getting antsy in my chair. My feet started tapping a million miles a minute, so I got up and started looking around the farmers market. There was a little jewelry stand run by two older ladies. I had a little pin from my birthday that Aunt Val gave me on my jacket, and the two ladies wouldn't stop babbling about it for some reason. I was looking around their little table of homemade bracelets and rings, and I fell in love with a thin gold ring that had your birthstone in it.

I haggled with the women to get that ring. After a few minutes of going back and forth with each other, I traded them my birthday pin and your bracelet for the ring. Mama, you would just love it. It's so small and plain, but a pretty plain. I was playing with the ring in my hands and then Vera called me over because she was about to start her mini-performance. I could've listened to her sing my least favorite song in the whole wide world and I would still be mesmerized by her pretty voice. Even if she wasn't a good singer, watching her effortlessly strum her guitar was the most satisfying I ever did see. I didn't even realize she finished singing, I was just staring into space. I finally snapped out of it when I heard the people around us start cheering for her. She counted up the tips in her guitar case and she only had about nine dollars, including the change I threw in there.

I helped her pack up her things and bring

them back to the van. She looked so discouraged with the amount she made, it hurt my heart real bad seeing her that way. I always saw you that way, and whenever I did I tried my best to cheer you up. Even though it never really worked with you, that's what I tried with Vera. I could tell her eyes were welling up so I knew I needed to act fast. I told her to stand in front of me. She hopped out of her van and seemed confused, which is what I expected. Then, I asked where her favorite place in the whole wide world was.

"Nashville, Tennessee." she said that without a second thought. Mama, I didn't even tell her that we lived there. I told you, we just have an instant connection, just like you and Daddy. I asked her to describe it to me a little bit more. The words rolled right off her tongue, it was like she saw that question coming. She described it with the most vivid words that you would've thought she was talking about heaven, not an old town in Nashville.

After she was done explaining, I just looked at her for a second. I looked at her pretty hair, her pretty plain outfit, and her pretty eyes that matched my new ring. There was just something about her that was comforting, which is why it was so easy to trust her. I told her that we were from Nashville, and she was amazed. She was confused as to how I ended up in Vermont, so I told her everything I knew. I told her Daddy was gone. I told you that you were still here, but it felt like you were gone. I told her that after Daddy was buried here near Aunt Val's house, I didn't see you again. I told her how I would get to see you soon, though. The last thing I told her about was how much I miss Nashville and how badly I want to go back to see you there since you haven't been getting my letters. Then, I asked her what made Nashville her favorite place.

She told me everything Mama, everything. When her family was stationed in Tennessee, Vera's younger sister Emily fell in love with it and wanted to stay there forever. When Emily got sick, her parents said that she needed better doctors, so her dad asked for them to get stationed in Vermont, where they had a really good program for kids with cancer. Vera told me that Emily passed away about a month after moving to Vermont. Not long after that, her dad had to go to Iraq, and he's still there. She didn't want to talk about it much, but her mama also passed away.

I asked her if she remembers where they used to live in Nashville. She just nodded. I didn't mean for her to get more upset. I started to think that I made things worse. After a few minutes of awkward silence, Vera looked up at me.

"Do you like adventures?" she said, it sounded as if she already cheered up.

I just nodded because I didn't want my words to make her sad. She didn't say anything after that, she just told me to get in the van because we were going home. We wouldn't have been in this awkward situation if it weren't for me asking about Nashville. When she dropped me off, I gave her a hug, but I felt terrible. Yesterday started so good, but I ruined it by trying to cheer her up, just like I used to do with you. It's okay, though. I'm seeing her again tomorrow, maybe things will be better by then. I kept my distance today. I'll keep you updated.

Faithfully,

Cove

September 28, 2004

Dear Mama,

This letter might be short because I'm getting ready for bed. Today was really good. I was still sad about yesterday, and I felt mighty guilty, but I think I'm okay now. Vera came to the house pretty early, I was still in my jammies and I was eating breakfast with Aunt Val. She told me to get dressed because we were going on the adventure she was asking about the last time we saw each other. As I was leaving the room, I saw Aunt Val gesture toward a chair at the kitchen table for Vera to sit at. It made me feel all warm inside. I was happy that Aunt Val liked Vera since they both meant a lot to me.

I went in our room to get changed, but I heard Aunt Val and Vera babbling to each other, so I got that warm feeling again which cheered me up. I wore that dress you gave me a few years ago, the flowy sage one that has daisies on it. I forgot about it, but Aunt Val must've done the laundry so it was laid out on the bed. Aunt Val wanted me to start sleeping in her room with her. I wasn't able to sleep through the night anymore. I would wake up sweaty or shivering and my head would be spinning. Aunt Val talked to Mr. Graves about it, though. He said that it was normal, though. It was just because I was missing you and Daddy, that's all. So now Aunt Val wants me to sleep in bed with her, she said it'll make me feel less lonely at night.

After I got dressed, I walked back out into the kitchen. Aunt Val told me the color matched my eyes which made me smile. Vera sat across from her with a smirk on her face. Aunt Val fixed everyone up a cup of coffee.

"Vera tells me you guys are goin' somewhere." Aunt Val said. I didn't know what to say because she never mentioned leaving to go anywhere. I just made a confused face and then Vera held up a Dollywood t-shirt. I asked if I was dreaming. It sure felt like I was. I was gonna be able to go on a road trip with my best friend to see you Mama! My hand covered my mouth because I was in such shock.

"We can leave tonight and be there tomorrow morning. We can stay however long you want, Co. We'll visit your mom and I'll bring you to all the places Emily and I used to go to. Deal?" Vera was beaming. Her smile was so sincere, the warm feeling was constant now. I started nodding because I couldn't figure out what to say and I didn't want to start rambling on about nonsense. I grabbed Vera's hand and we ran into my room to start packing. I packed up just about all the clothes I had. We decided to leave tomorrow morning. I'm not sure how long I'll be away from Aunt Val, but I don't want to hurt her heart, so I'm spending tonight with her while Vera gets the van ready for a road trip. We'll watch *Punky Brewster* reruns because I know I'll miss watching them with her while I'm gone. I told Vera we'll have to stop at the post office on the way so I can keep you updated. Aunt Val called my school and told them I wouldn't be going anymore. I never cared for that place anyway. I'll see you soon Mama, real soon.

Unapologetically,

Cove

See you later, Vera

October 1st, 2004

Dear Daddy,

I'm not sure if you read or even received my letter, but life seems so unreal that I have to write it and send it somewhere, no matter who is reading. For a while, my life was at such an all time low, all I needed was someone, anyone. For being so young, I didn't think I'd ever feel the way I did a few weeks ago. Meeting Cove was such a pivotal moment in my life, I'm on a roller coaster that only goes up. We took a road trip to Nashville, I tried to drive all the way through, but we had to make a few stops. Cove wanted to send letters to her mom and her aunt to keep them updated, so we had to stop at some post offices. I didn't mind, though.

We also stopped a few times to eat. Her aunt gave us some money from the swear jar that she had for a few years. She sure must have a mouth on her, 500 dollars worth of words. This made the drive so much more special. I was worried that Cove would want to just turn around at some point because we wouldn't be able to eat three meals a day, or because I didn't have enough blankets for both of us to sleep with. Looking back at it, she wouldn't have cared about any of that. She's grateful for the little things. She's more emotionally invested in the moment than physically, just like Emily was.

One of the little pit stops we made was after about 10 hours of driving. I was craving ice cream, and so was she. The sun was starting to set, and we didn't want to freeze from the October breeze while we ate. We found a little Ma and Pa ice cream shop that sat on a boat pier in Kentucky. We were both able to get our own thanks to the money her aunt gave us. We sat on the pier with our legs dangling over the water with the sun setting in front of us. It was like we were in a movie. I haven't felt such an ethereal feeling of happiness like that in months. It was the refresher I needed. Cove was babbling about whatever came to her mind, mostly about how long it had been since she had ice cream that good.

Sometimes when she's talking, I just stare. I'm just mesmerized. It's a feeling I can't explain. I was still deciphering if it was platonic or not, I've never been good at comprehending my emotions.

We met a week ago, but it felt like an eternity, an eternity that could never be long enough. We were having a conversation about every little thing we thought of. Our favorite colors, aspirations, and interests. She's such a fragile person. It was like someone broke her and glued her back together, but the glue wasn't dry yet. She was still a little bit cautious about telling me random little things. I didn't pressure her, though, I saw her fragility as a strength.

She was losing part of her positivity, though. When we first met, she had such a spark of optimism that it was almost blinding. One of the things she's nervous about telling me about is her mom. She writes letters to her mom who lives in Nashville, but still hasn't gotten an answer. That's what sealed the deal on this road trip. I wanted to reminisce and go to Dollywood, Emily's favorite place, and Cove wanted to go see her mom. Though I try my best to stay optimistic for her, this situation makes it a bit difficult. She has so much faith in her mom, just like I did. I just hope she doesn't get her heart broken.

The night on the pier was such a dream, it made me remember why the connection was instant. The simplicity of her words didn't match the complication of her thoughts, something I thought only I experienced. When she was talking and I just stared, I could tell she was thinking hard. I couldn't tell what she was thinking about, but it meant something to her. She always referred to her negative thoughts as demons, so they must've been dancing around in her complicated mind. I was wearing your fleece-lined cargo jacket that was about three sizes too big for me. It smelled like those fancy cigars you and Uncle Roger always had over the summer, it was so nostalgic. I carried Emily's locket with me everywhere, mine was usually around my neck and hers was in my pocket 99% of the time. I told Cove to close her eyes, a strategy she used on me when she saw me feeling gloomy.

Her eyes were closed, so I reached in the pocket of your huge jacket and shuffled around the receipts and took out the locket. I told Cove to open her eyes, and when she did, she immediately knew what I was holding up. She held her hair up and I put it around her neck. Our expressions did the talking at this point. We both were tearing up, but I wanted to save my tears for an appropriate time. Cove just raised her eyes to the pink sky to stop the tears from getting out. We both smiled at each other and she leaned her head on my shoulder, a picture perfect moment. We're getting ready to go to sleep, and we'll see her mom on the way to Dollywood tomorrow. Both of our stomachs are cluttered with butterflies, just like the butterfly on Emily's locket. Wherever Emily may be, I hope she's smiling.

Xoxo,

Vera

October 5th, 2004

Dear Daddy,

You won't get the chance to read this, but you're watching me write it. The ethereal happiness has come to an end, just like everything else. Cove and I got to her mother's house, where we were greeted by a huge pile of letters in front of the door addressed to "Mama Collins," along with an array of eviction notices on the door. I feared for what we were about to see, and I feared for how Cove would react, and how her mind would react. I walked up to the door and looked back at Cove for reassurance that I should be the one knocking on the door. She looked so excited, I'm still unsure if she knew whose letters those were. Either way, she picked all of them up and cradled them as I knocked on the door.

I heard the deadbolt unlock with hesitation. Cove was ready to explode with excitement. The door slowly creaked open and we were awkwardly greeted by a man that seemed to be about 40. He had a musk surrounding him, almost like Pigpen from Charlie Brown. He had a cigarette burning in his hand as he looked the both of us up and down. Cove's smile turned more neutral, and I backed up a few steps and wrapped my arm around hers. We both needed the security. There was a raspy muffled voice coming from behind the man who just awkwardly stood there. Nobody said anything. He looked like he knew who Cove was, but I'm not sure if she knew him.

The raspy voice was becoming more

apparent, and suddenly the voice had a face. A woman stumbled past the man standing in the doorway, barely being able to stand on her own two feet. Her hair was matted, but she had the same olive skin tone as Cove and the same emerald eyes. Cove now stood there in disbelief. I'm surprised the stench of poor hygiene and cigarettes didn't overcome her.

"So this is the life you traded me for?" that's all Cove said, that's all that needed to be said in order for her mother to erupt. Her barely sober mother turned beet red from embarrassment and anger. She struggled to speak coherently at all, but continued to yell at Cove with her best efforts. She was saying how Cove is the reason she has this life, I stood next to Cove, and I felt her trembling and I was biting my tongue.

"You must take your uselessness after your dad," her mother said this so confidently that I realized I had been quiet long enough. I unhooked my arm from Cove's and took the letters from her. I ripped the letter out of a shredded envelope and read the first part my eyes glanced at.

"'My birthday is only two days away., I hope to see you there. I'm visiting Daddy to talk to him for a little bit in the morning and then Aunt Val said we can go to Blockbuster and pick out a few movies or CDs to watch that night. I'll be sure to pick up The Wizard of Oz.' See ma'am, I think you've confused compassion and uselessness, maybe you used those words on the wrong people." I went on such a tangent, almost a monologue.

When I was finished, Cove was in tears and her mother stared at me. I threw the letters on the ground and shuffled around my pockets for one of your old lighters. Once I found it, I set the pile of letters on fire. I was worried if Cove was going to be angry with me for this, but then I remembered who I was dealing with. Cove came from behind me and ripped an eviction notice off the front door, waved it in her mother's face, and threw it into the fire. Lastly, she took the cigarette out of the man's hand and put it out on the front door, leaving a small burn mark.

Cove abruptly turned around and grabbed my hand, we started walking back to the van as her mother started babbling some swear words I'd never heard before.

"Daddy would be saying the same thing to you right now!" Cove shouted as we got to the van.

I was so proud. I didn't think she would ever get frustrated like that, but I guess the demons were composed of anger that was built up. The first half of the car ride was silent. Then, out of thin air, Cove started apologizing. She turned into a puddle of regret, but I reassured her that it would've happened either way, and that she should be so proud of herself. She was so utterly grateful for me being there. Honestly, I'm not sure if she would've been able to do this herself, so I'm happy I was there too.

I didn't bother stopping at Dollywood, I needed to get Cove to her aunt as soon as possible. We hardly stopped on this drive back, I lived off of copious amounts of coffee to drive straight to Vermont and Cove pondered and wrote in her little notebook most of the drive. I mainly thought about the few lines about me I saw when I was scrambling to find a line to read from the letter to her mom. It's good to know this feeling is reciprocated. It's not something I'm used to.

We finally got back to her apartment complex and I was gathering her things to help her bring them back inside. Cove was leaned up against the van until she tapped my shoulder. When I turned around, there were two men from the Marine Corps walking up to me. I started hyperventilating and I didn't think it could be real until one of them said, "Vera Baron, it's with deep sorrow that we tell y-"

I didn't let him finish. I covered my face and screamed as I fell to my knees. I heard Cove's aunt running out of their apartment as Cove got to my level and hugged me as tight as she could. The men got down to our level as well and placed your uniform and cap in front of me with a letter neatly folded on top. Your chicken scratch handwriting spelled out my name on the front, but I'm still not ready to read it.

Life fell through the cracks of my fingers so quickly. I still haven't comprehended your death, but I know you're up there with Emily, which is all I could ever ask for. I wish I wrote to you sooner, and I wish I hugged you longer. This letter will just stay tucked away somewhere, but I know you watched me write it. Wherever you may be, I need your guidance. Please don't let Cove leave, I need her like the air just about now.

See you later,

Vera

Farewell,
Cove

October 8th, 2004

Dear whoever finds this letter,

I'm not sure who is going to find my letter first, but I'll mention everyone that I think might care. My decision was only made by me, it's not anyone's fault but my own. Since I was young, I've always been positive. When you're put in situations like mine, you don't really have a choice but to put on a brave face and pretend everything's alright. I can't explain how I felt very well. In a sense, I felt homesick of a place that never existed. A place where I always felt the warmth I felt when I was with Vera, a place where the kitchen smelled like dinner in the oven instead of bleach, just a place that felt like home instead of just four walls. I wanted to feel the fuzzy feeling I felt around Vera

all the time, not the cold lonely feeling I had whenever I was around anyone else.

I've been told by so many people that the pain would pass and for a split second, it did. For that whole split second, I was with Vera, and I felt the most comfortable and warm than I have ever felt. It was like Vera just had a little bit of light with her wherever she went and sprinkled it all over me when we were together. Our time here was limited, but I hope to see her again another time.

Thinking about how my actions are the reason I'm so upset with myself makes me cringe. I don't know why I am this way, it's like I'm programmed to mess things up. Whoever is reading this might think that these little things aren't my fault, but they completely are. There's a reason for Mama not wanting me, it's my personality. There's a reason I never felt good enough for Vera, it's my everything. She was the definition of ethereality, a word she taught me that is so beautiful that I can only use it to describe her, an otherworldly type of beauty.

Mama, I'm sorry for whatever I did to you. I wish I knew exactly what I did, but it's too late for closure and it would only hurt me more. When Vera and I got home from Tennessee, I didn't even find the time to tell Aunt Val what happened because I had to comfort Vera while she grieved. I'm sorry for whatever I did to you, whatever that may be. I'm not mad at you at all, just myself for not being able to be loved by my own mama.

Aunt Val, you were amazing. It was a

surprise to you that I'd be your new roommate, and you tried your very best to make sure that I was happy. Thank you for being the one to stick around for me when Mama wasn't able to and eventually didn't want to. I'm sorry if you're the one that found me in the bathroom because you tried your best to give me the world, even if you only had Pluto to offer. Wherever I am, I'm sending all of my love to you.

Vera, you are the love of my life. I'm sorry things had to be this way, but I had to do this for you more than anyone. I didn't want to hurt you the way everyone else in your life has, which is one of the reasons I did this. I don't know if you left town after we came home to just take a break from the world, or to leave me behind, but both are understandable. I didn't want to be the reason you stayed in this ghost town. Wherever you are, I know you're going to do great things for yourself and the people in your life that you have left.

One of the leading things that brought me to this decision was that I would never meet another person like Vera. The only time I didn't have to wear a mask of happiness was when I was around her, and after she left town I didn't know if I would get to feel that happiness again. It wasn't a chance I was willing to take. I know it seems selfish of me but the feeling of being unwanted that Mama made me feel greatly was so unbearable. I've never put so much faith into someone just to get turned down until then, but I guess I did the same to her so I was getting a taste of my own medicine.

I hope I'm with Daddy now. I also hope I get to meet Vera's parents and Emily. Most importantly, I hope I get to see Vera from where I am. I want to see her living the dreams she was too nervous to tell me about because she didn't want to fail me by not achieving them. Whatever she does in life, I hope she knows that I'll be so proud of her, whether that information is useful to her or not. Although I'm proud of her, I know she won't be proud of the decision I made. At the very least, I hope she understands my decision. Vera was just so much more than a person, she's the one that always brought me back down to Earth when I needed it, she was just too late this time. Nobody ever stood up for me the way she did against Mama, not even

Daddy.

The demons became too much for me to handle. I was raised to never play the victim but it's difficult not to do so when all the demons do is tell you things that make your head spin. I wish I knew what was wrong with me and why I felt like this all the time. I'm sure that while you are reading this you're thinking about how none of these tragedies are my fault, but the demons told me everything was my fault, therefore it is. A lot of people liked to believe I don't understand what's going on, oftentimes I don't, but I did most of the time, I was just afraid of letting go.

The one thing I refused to believe from the demons was that Mama wasn't coming back. In my heart, I knew she wasn't, but I hoped my letters would make her want me again. Mama, if you're reading this, nothing is your fault. I take the blame for thinking you even loved me to begin with. One of the things I regret doing the most is not figuring out who that man with you was, and why you're choosing to hurt him as well. I woke up one day expecting to bring you home to Aunt Val with Vera, but left with a silent car ride home where I pretended to sleep so I didn't need to talk. The embarrassment was too much for me to talk about. Vera's heart is too big for her body, so she drove all the way here just so I could see you, and she skipped going to visit her late sister's favorite place just so we could go home and see Aunt Val.

I know my words and regards are all over the place, and I'm sorry for that. I have so much to say but I'm not sure if I have enough paper or time left before Aunt Val gets home from work. Mr. Greeves is going to be mighty disappointed in me, but I hope he understands that I didn't just make this a snap decision. I've been thinking about it the past few days. Well, since Aunt Val told me Mr. Greeves called to tell her that Vera quit her job. He explained that the only context she gave was that she needed a break. He also said she wasn't very cordial about it, whatever that means. Aunt Val told me that Mr. Greeves sounded worried, but that's because he doesn't know how Vera is. I'm not completely worried about where Vera is or how she's doing because she's always been good at being on her own, I just wish she talked to me a little bit about this.

I know people are going to be affected by my death, but soon they'll realize how it was more of a pro than a con for me to be out of their lives. I was an unneeded burden, kind of just a bomb that would go off soon enough and destroy everything around me. I didn't want to be the reason everyone was walking on eggshells to avoid a bomb that would be going off soon, so that's why I decided to take myself out of everyone's equation. My one wish is that Aunt Val spares you the details of what I did and how I did it, because I didn't know any other way.

I want to be buried, just a tiny service with Vera, Mr. Greeves, and Aunt Val. I want to be buried in Emily's locket to prove how appreciative I am of being able to have it. Nobody's ever done something like that for me. I also want to be buried in the daisy dress if that's possible. Lastly, please let me lay next to Daddy, I wouldn't want to be by anyone else's side.

They say you aren't supposed to die with regrets, but I had to escape those regrets. The only thing that kept me here this long was Vera, and before I met Vera, it was the thought of meeting someone like her. I don't know how she felt. We talked about our feelings, but not feelings toward each other. I always thought of my future when I was a little girl. I thought about how I'd have a husband and kids. Now, the only person I'd want to spend the rest of my life with is Vera. I wish I hugged her longer because I don't think she knew it would be the last time.

I'm so sorry to anyone this decision is negatively affecting, but understand it was for your own good as well as mine. Over time, things lose meaning to people, no matter how big or small. Although it was abrupt, life to me lost its meaning. All of my actions were done with love and truth, not morality.

Farewell,

Cove Valentina Collins

Xoxo,
Vera

October 15th, 2004

Dear Cove,

I promise there's a good explanation as to why I left town. It's not your fault in the slightest, I just had to get away from reality for a few days. I'll be back in the beginning of November and I promise we can go on way more adventures with much happier endings.

When I got in my van to leave, I didn't even know where I was going. I just had to leave Vermont for a little while to clear my head. My first stop was my old house. I wanted to see if anyone lived there, and if they made it a home instead of just a house without any warmth. The for sale sign had a sold sticker on it, which was a bittersweet feeling. The last time I had all of my family members in one house was there, but they were all in the worst shape of their lives. The bitter part comes from seeing them in that condition, but the sweet part is to new beginnings, with you.

I'm sorry for this letter being overdue, I know I should've given you an explanation even before I left. I've never been good at showing how I feel, especially when it comes to loss. I've lost so many people within the last year but I never had anyone to talk to about it, so it was just unresolved nonsense going on in my head. When I come back from my mini excursion, I'll tell you everything. No more secrets about how I feel, how my life is, and how my life was. You deserve so much more than what I'm giving you. You deserve so much more than what anyone's giving you. You're impossibly optimistic, it's incredible.

In a little over a week, it'll be one month since your birthday party. I still remember the first time I saw you in that cheesy support group. I remember seeing you play with the ends of your hair every time we made eye contact. I can't even explain how I felt. I'd like to put it more abstractly than flatout saying we had a connection, but it's unfair to compare the feeling I got when I saw you to anything else. Simply because no matter how abstractly I put it, it'll never meet up to my standards. I'm always standoffish with new people, so I was hoping you would talk to me first because I wouldn't be able to work up the courage to talk to you myself.

Although I mentioned the connection I felt,

I didn't think we would get this far. For knowing each other for such a short amount of time, it's like we've known each other for years. I've never felt this comfortable with anyone, not even my own sister (she was a very close second, though.) To be completely honest, I didn't expect much to come out of this friendship. In my mind, I was giving it a week, but I was hoping it would be much longer than that because again, my intuition told me you were different from everyone else. Your persistence made me feel so much more comfortable with myself, and just made me feel more wanted.

My time with my family was cut so short, that the feeling of being wanted by someone was so foreign to me, especially because in the final days of being with my family as a whole, we didn't feel like a family, we felt like strangers. I'm sorry if my emotions are a bit overbearing, it's just difficult to put into words. Before I dropped out of school, I had to talk to countless amounts of counselors and I got no benefit from any of them. They only talked to me for a paycheck, but you're the most selfless person I've ever met. Every time we talked, as cliche as it sounds, I knew it came from your heart.

I'm sorry for putting all of my feelings out there at once, but you need an explanation more than anyone else. You're the only person I've ever cared about not disappointing. After I lost Emily, I've always tried my best to avoid associating people with so much emotion. For a while, it worked, but then we met.

I've never had the pleasure of confiding in

someone so much, and I was so worried that you would get tired of me relatively quickly, but that fear went away after your birthday. Whenever we're together, I feel infinite. There's no other way to put it. There aren't any worries. Of course, there are ups and downs sometimes but I've only been confident in us moving past the bad parts.

Truthfully, Cove, this is the feeling I see people attempt to portray in movies. This feeling is so much better to live through than to watch on a screen. Thinking about it, our month-long adventure belongs in a movie. Except in the movie, the ending is always happy but the plot makes it seem like it won't be. I know this letter seems like a cluster of thought, and that's because it is. Everything that's coming to mind, I'm just writing down. You're the first to know that I have a habit of rambling when I've got a lot on my mind, which is why I'm okay with sending you this messy, sappy, whirlwind of a letter.

By the time you get this, I'll most likely be in Nashville. I decided to go back so I could see Emily's favorite destinations. While I wish I brought you with me, this is also time I need to myself. I loved spending nearly everyday with you, I just needed some time to recuperate after I found out about my dad. I hope you don't think my decision is selfish. I promise I'll be back soon. In the meantime, here are some things I've been needing to tell you.

Not to make this even cheesier, but I love you. There's no way to put that more delicately.

I've never been able to express that type of emotion very well either, as you can tell. I don't even mean that in a romantic way, I just have so much love for you as a best friend, that there's no other phrase strong enough to convey that. For the most part, we're alike. The biggest difference though is that I'm the pessimist and you're the optimist. We're like Yin and Yang, a relationship I haven't felt since Emily was still around. The difference with that, though, is that Emily lost her sense of optimism within her last few days, you have yet to lose it and I hope you never do.

I have a habit of biting the bullet and accepting what happens to me, you persevere. I've never seen anyone as strong as you. This whole time we've been around each other, I've been wondering why you store so much faith in me, but I think I finally figured it out. You treat people in such a way that you never received when you were younger. We grew up having our teachers tell us to "treat people the way you want to be treated," and I think you ran with that philosophy, which is beautifully upsetting.

I try my best to avoid being the victim, but it's only right for me to be upfront with you. I've dealt with so much loss in my life and I know that I pretended as if I didn't care or impulsively did something irrational, for example, the situation I'm in right now. Everything is so different when it comes to you. I'd dance to the end of the world with you if it meant you never had to leave. I'm sorry if I come off as stuck up for not physically showing my emotion to you, or being quiet whenever you talk. I'm so invested in everything you say, it's captivating. At first I felt bad getting lost in your words, but then I realized you do the same.

Whatever this is that we have between us, I'd love to keep it forever. People often preach about how good change is, but it's so overrated. I don't want my life to change anymore than it already has. It took for me to lose nearly everything to put my life into perspective, I can't afford for anything else to change. Not now, at least. The day I lose you, I'll lose myself. I had a preview of this feeling when I lost Emily, but now I know it'll be real if I ever lose you. I didn't know who I was when I went through the cycle of grief, rebellion, and healing. With you, there's not going to be any healing. I'm not even sure if there's going to be rebellion either, I won't know what to do with myself.

Alright, I think I'm done with the sad stuff, you get the point. I just needed you to know that you're always going to be in my heart, even though I'm out of town for a little while. I've always distanced myself from the people I care most about, I never would've thought I'd change. Again, though, you've helped me get through that so much. I know I can be myself around you, and that's all I could ever ask for.

The love I have for you is otherworldly, or your new favorite word, ethereal. I truly need you to know that. You've brought nothing but the utmost joy to my life, and I can't thank you enough. I just wish Emily was around to meet you, you would've loved each other. When I get back, we can go to the farmers market and you can spend your allowance on things you don't need. We can get you a sleeping bag for my van so you can travel with me more comfortably. We can watch Punky Brewster with your amazing Aunt Val. When I get back, it'll be a fresh start, one that we both needed. I'll be at your door in the morning of November first, bright and early. We can start our next adventure from there. We have the rest of our lives to plan out, I wouldn't want anyone else by my side.

Xoxo,

Vera

Epilogue

Dear Vera,

I'm not sure how long it's been or what day you're opening this, but that's not very important. As long as you found these, that's all that matters. There's a box under the bed that has more letters and more of the explanations that you need and deserve.

I'm sorry if this is happening too quickly for you, but I'll help you as much as I can. Well, as much as I thought was appropriate. I know you have tons of questions, I tried my best to answer them all. I hope my best was enough, because it never seemed to be.

Hugs from above

Author's Note

This story's original purpose was for my creative writing class. A quote my teacher tended to throw around was to, "Write what you know." I began living by this motto whenever I was writing. As I was brainstorming the traits of Vera and Cove, I realized that they both had major aspects of me in them. While I've never gone through a majority of the conflicts they go through in this story, I've experienced every emotion described because I was only writing what I know.

I've never felt so connected to my own characters this intensely before. During the writing process, my teacher would ask why certain characters made some of the decisions they did. Since it was as if I knew these characters inside out, I often forgot that people didn't understand my characters as much as I did.

A person's worst mistake is comparing their own tragedies to someone else's. So, while some people may think that Cove's actions were outlandish considering all of the horrid events Vera has gone through, that doesn't lessen the gravity of Cove's trauma. As people we have grown up being told that there are people going through much more than what we are, and that it could always be worse. By living with that thought at the back of our minds, we seem to lose ourselves because we're worried about other people's' problems that we don't even know of, yet compare their life to ours. I used this thought process as one of the few skeletons in Vera's closet.

As for Cove, I think everyone has had those few bitter moments of feeling at your peak when it comes to inner faith, then having it all plummet. I don't mean anything religious by this, I mean the inner intuition, or a gut feeling of faith that your mind creates rather than a higher power.

I always found myself comparing Cove to a window. Her fragility is apparent, but her surface is difficult to scratch. Vera, on the other hand is the opposite to an extent. Her surface is scratched far beyond compare, but she'll never break.

I sincerely thank you for coming on this journey with Cove and Vera. In my heart, I know they would've appreciated it. Vera will be back soon.